the
Little Book

of Stupid
Questions

the Little Book of Stupid Questions

300 Hilarious, Bold, Embarrassing, Personal and Basically Pointless Queries

David Borgenicht

 Hysteria

A Division of Sourcebooks, Inc.

Naperville, IL • Bridgeport, CT

Published by Hysteria, a division of Sourcebooks, Inc.

Naperville Office   Bridgeport Office
P.O. Box 372   955 Connecticut Ave. #1209
Naperville, IL 60566   Bridgeport, CT 06607
(630) 961-3900   (203) 333-9399
Fax: (630) 961-2168   Fax: (203) 367-7188

ISBN 1-887166-50-5

Printed and bound in the United States of America
10   9   8   7   6   5   4   3   2   1

Dedication

To Groucho, Chico, and Harpo—My Mentors

Acknowledgments

Many thanks to Jim Grace and Virginia Mattingly for their help in creating this book. Your stupidity is exceeded only by my own.

The Stupid Introduction

Think of this book as a new beginning.

Philosophers throughout the ages have been tackling the big, meaningful questions of the universe. "Why are we here?" "Is there life after death?" "What is love?" They haven't come up with any real answers yet, but the questions have been debated to death, from Ancient Greece to the modern day.

And I'm sick of it. Who cares why we're here? What matters is what we do with our time while we're here. Who cares if there's life after death? We can't take it with us. And who knows what love is? I don't even understand how a thermos works. I just

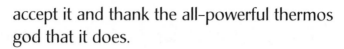

accept it and thank the all-powerful thermos god that it does.

You see, from day to day, we don't deal with these major metaphysical issues. We deal with the little things. The inane things. The petty things. And yes, well, the stupid things.

We ask ourselves ridiculous questions about our bodies, our friends, our families. Questions about TV shows, and movies, and music. Questions about belly buttons, and airplane crashes, and sex, and elevators, and spontaneous combustion, and dozens of other incredibly silly but immensely interesting subjects.

And it's time we had an international forum on these subjects as well. It's time we focused on the issues we all really talk about when we're out with friends or standing around the watercooler at work.

This book will help us to start that dialogue. Within it are hundreds of stupid questions, all of them quite worthy of discussion, and all with no right or wrong answers to worry about. That, I leave up to you.

Leave the book anywhere you want meaningless thoughts and conversation inspired. The bathroom. The kitchen table. The car. The liquor cabinet. Talk amongst yourselves. And think before you speak.

As you're discussing the questions within, you'll likely come up with your own stupid thoughts and issues. My hope is that this book will inspire such a renaissance of stupid dialogue. So as you come up with your own questions, send them to me. You can reach me via email at davidaborg@aol.com, or through the publisher (see the copyright page for their address). I'm already working on another volume, and if your questions

are just stupid enough, I might include them, and you'll receive a hearty "thanks" and a free copy of the next volume.

But until then, free up your mind of any deep thoughts. Get ready to get real.

And to get stupid.

David Borgenicht, 1999

the Little Book of Stupid Questions

√If you had a third eye, where would you
put it?

If you could have an extra appendage, what
would it be and where would you put it?

If you could trade one body part with anyone you know, what would it be, and with whom would you trade?

Do you ever make faces behind people's backs? Do you think they ever make faces at you?

Do you consider yourself well endowed? What animal would you say you're "hung like"?

Why don't men "do" their hair more often or wear makeup? If it makes women look better, wouldn't it make men look better, too?

Is it weirder for you to make love in your parents' bedroom or for your parents to make love in your bedroom?

If you were a porn star, what would your name be? What would you be known for?

Who's the better boyfriend—Kramer, George, or Jerry? Who's the better girlfriend—Monica, Rachel, or Phoebe?

Which *Brady Bunch* family member would you most like to see naked? Least like?

Which *Brady Bunch* family member would you most like to be?

If your bologna had a first name what would it be? What about your other cold cuts?

? ¿ ?

"Only two things are infinite, the universe and human stupidity—and I'm not sure about the former."

—*Albert Einstein*

? ¿ ?

Why does everyone move around when someone steps out of an elevator? Do we think it might collapse?

When someone enters a building in front of you and holds the door open, do you feel compelled to rush through it so that they aren't waiting for you? Why do we do this, especially when it's someone we don't know?

Would life be simpler if we could settle adult disputes the same way we did when we were kids—by "calling it," by pushing and shoving (but never really seriously injuring), and by invoking the "no give-backs" rule?

Would you rather have "Oh, Mickey," "Cars," or "Manic Monday" stuck in your head?

What superpowers do you have if you are a supermodel?

If, by some quirk of fate, you run into your favorite celebrity/supermodel fantasy object, and, by some other quirk of fate, they come on to you, what would you do? What if you were in a committed relationship? Do you ask for an autograph afterwards?

Who do you know that is most likely to not wear any underwear? Most likely not to change their underwear daily?

Who do you know that is most likely to visit a prostitute? Would you ever be one (think worst-case scenario here)? Would you ever be an exotic dancer? What would you call yourself?

Did you cry more in *E.T.*, *Schindler's List*, *Platoon*, or *Forrest Gump*? What was the most recent movie you cried in? Were you alone?

What is the strangest thing you've ever eaten? How did it originally live (or how was it originally used)?

When you're in the shower and you see a little hair on the tile wall, do you fill your hands with water and try to splash it off, or try to pluck it off with your fingers? Why are we so predictable?

Why do you think Charlie needed Angels? Can you think of any reason that you'd need them? Can you think of any reason you wouldn't? (Note: a "jiggle-fix" is not a reason)

Would you rather be lost in space or lost on an uncharted desert isle? What if you were lost in space with Tom Cruise or Elle McPherson, or left on a desert isle with Tom Bosley or "Fat" Elvis?

✓If you were lost on a desert island and could take with you one book, one CD (they have a player there), and one outfit, what would you choose?

? ¿ ?

"Everybody is ignorant, only on different subjects."

—Will Rogers

? ¿ ?

Why is it called a navel? Do you think people with "innies" are more introverted than people with "outies"? Does the shape of your navel have anything to do with your sea worthiness?

Can you think of a way, within six steps or less, to connect yourself to Kevin Bacon? What about Francis Bacon? Canadian Bacon?

? ¿ ?

"There is no limit to stupidity. Space itself is said to be bounded by its own curvature, but stupidity continues beyond infinity."

—*Gene Wolfe*

? ¿ ?

Who was tougher, Starsky or Hutch? Simon or Simon? Cagney or Lacey?

Do you believe honesty is the best policy? If so, is it wrong to fake your emotions in bed?

Can men fake it? Should they?

Would the world be a better place if skipping were more common than walking? (Issues to consider: more scrapes and bruises, better aerobic health, better spirits, more lost keys)

When you're on the road and someone cuts you off, do you ever mouth a curse at him or her through the window without actually speaking? Why? Does this make you feel better?

If your house was on fire and you could only grab one thing to take with you, what would it be? (Hint for men: Don't forget about your significant others)

What vegetable do you most resemble?
What about your friends?

Who's more likely to catch a crook, the officers of CHiPs, the officers of Miami Vice, or the officers of Hill Street?

Are you more likely to be the "good cop" or the "bad cop"?

Do you think you've learned enough about emergency medicine from TV to save someone who has flatlined right in front of you? Could you use one of those "clear" machines? Could you perform an emergency tracheotomy?

If you were infected by a deadly biochemical and the only way to survive was to take one of those huge cardiac needles and plunge it through your sternum right into your heart, would you be able to save yourself?

What would your name be if you were a goodfella? (Example: David "The Schnoz" Borgenicht) Do you think you could break someone's leg if you really had to? Why do mafia types have such nice clothes, but such tacky interior décor?

Can you name two people you really don't ever want to picture making love? Describe their passionate encounter in vivid detail.

Can you name two people who you think are the perfect couple? Remember, "perfect couple" could mean that you'd never wish either of them on anyone else.

What part of your body do you wish were bigger? Smaller? A different color?

Which celebrity's butt would you most like to squeeze? Which celebrity would you most like to have squeeze your butt?

Which cartoon character do you most resemble? What about your friends?

Which cartoon ability would you rather have—the ability to paint a hole in the ground or a door in a solid wall and go through it, the ability to be run over by a steamroller and shake yourself back to normal, or the ability to fall hundreds of feet off a cliff to your doom and be back in the very next scene?

If a store overcharges you for an item, is it wrong to shoplift something of equivalent value? What about buying a dress or piece of jewelry, wearing it to an event, and then returning it?

What dead person would you LEAST want to be haunted by? (Key factor: how they died will affect how they look as a ghost)

Who would you rather have operate on you, the cast of *ER*, the cast of *Quincy*, or the cast of *M*A*S*H*? (Key factors: cleanliness, bedside manner, ability to assess what went wrong afterwards)

Who would you rather date, Betty or Veronica? Archie or Reggie? Wonder Woman or Batgirl? Spiderman or Batman? Ginger or Maryann? Gilligan or the Professor? Magnum P.I. or Dan Tanna? Who would you rather sleep with?

If you could have a one night stand with any one of five celebrities (assuming they were willing), which five would you choose?

Which celebrity do you think you have the most realistic chance of having a meaningful relationship with, and why?

Is life more like the game of Life, Sorry, or Monopoly?

? ¿ ?

"It costs to be stupid. The stupider you are, the more it costs."

—*Sherrill Brown*

? ¿ ?

Is business more like Risk or Battleship?

Does love really mean never having to say you're sorry, or does it really mean always having to say you're sorry? Is your answer different depending upon whether you're male or female?

Would you rather die by falling off a building into a river and drowning or by falling off a building into the pavement? (Key factors: open/closed casket, fear of heights)

You have a choice—you will be given the inestimable talents of either Yanni, Julio Iglesias, Lawrence Welk, Christopher Cross, or Michael Bolton. Whose talents do you select? What if to get those talents you also had to adopt their looks? Now whom would you choose?

? ¿ ?

"It is not clear that intelligence has any long-term survival value."

—Stephen Hawking

? ¿ ?

Would you accept the gift of always being able to have great sex if it meant that you would also always have a big, goofy grin on your face?

If you could give your partner extreme pleasure in bed simply by sneezing, would you do it, or would that be considered cheating?

If you could kill one person in the world simply by thinking of them and saying, "Buh-bye," would you do it? Who would you kill?

A twisted genie appears to you one day, and gives you the opportunity to have the writing talent of Stephen King, but the looks of David Crosby. Do you accept? What about the artistic talent of Jackson Pollack, but the looks of Richard Simmons?

Who would you most like to be stuck in an elevator with? Least like?

What is the strangest place you've ever been naked? Kissed

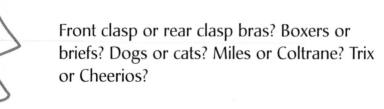

Front clasp or rear clasp bras? Boxers or briefs? Dogs or cats? Miles or Coltrane? Trix or Cheerios?

? ¿ ?

"Dare to be stupid!"

—Weird Al Yankovic

? ¿ ?

What breakfast cereal most describes your personality? (Key factors: remains crispy in milk, amount of sugar, vitamin fortification)

What era do you think you belong in (i.e., 1920s, 1940s, 1950s, 1980s, etc.)? What about your friends?

Who in your group of friends would you least like to see in lingerie? Most like? What about your family?

What do you think Victoria's secret is, and why won't she tell? Do you think it might be that she's really a lesbian?

Would you prefer your mate to be stupid and beautiful or intelligent and ugly? What about stupid, beautiful, and poor or intelligent, ugly, and rich?

If you were in prison for five years, how would you pass the time? What about twenty years? Life?

What famous person do you think you most resemble? What about your friends?

What famous person do other people tell you you most resemble?

Who would you most like to have a dream about tonight? What would you dream?

You are on a first date, and the person you are with has food stuck in his/her teeth. Would you tell him/her? What if they had food on their chin? Nose? Shirt?

If you could change your name, what would you pick?

If you were an animal, what kind would you be? A tree? A flower? A car?

Would you rather go a week without bathing, but be able to change your clothes, or a week without a change of clothes, but be able to bathe?

If all your underwear were dirty, would you go without, or wear a dirty pair? (Key factors: chafing, odor, likelihood of disrobing)

You are down to your last-last-last pair of underwear just before you do laundry—what does this pair look like?

? ¿ ?

"The two most common elements in the universe are hydrogen and stupidity."

—Harlan Ellison

? ¿ ?

Is it more time efficient to put on both socks and then both shoes, or one sock, one shoe and then the other sock, the other shoe?

What mail-order catalog would you be most likely to be a model for? What about your friends?

What do you think you will be doing at this exact moment twenty years from now?

If your life story were made into a movie, who would play you? Who would play your parents? Your best friend? What would it be called? Rated?

√If your life were made into a television show, would it be a soap opera, a drama, a sitcom? What would it be called?

Who do you know that would be the best talk show host? Who would be the best talk show guest?

Can you name five albums you owned when you were a teenager that you're embarrassed about now, but secretly enjoy?

Would you rather be a high-school
cheerleader or a professional cheerleader?

What musical group would you most likely
be a member of? What about your friends?

What TV character are you most like? What
about your friends?

If the Carnegie Deli named a sandwich in your honor, what would it be?

What is the correct order in which to wash your body when you're taking a shower?

If you were given a nickname, what would it be? What about your friends?

If you were a doughnut, what kind would you be? What about your friends?

Could God create a rock so heavy that he himself could not lift it? Remember, he is all-powerful.

If you ate your own foot, would you lose weight?

If cats and dogs didn't have fur would you still pet them, or would hamsters become more popular?

If your spouse killed someone, would you turn him or her in? What about your best friend? (Issue to consider: self-defense vs. premeditated)

How would you escape from a Turkish prison if wrongfully convicted?

Why do men have nipples?

Original Michael Jackson or Surgically-Altered Michael Jackson? Like a Virgin Madonna or Hindu Priestess Madonna? Beverly Hills Cop Eddie Murphy or Dr. Doolittle Eddie Murphy? Throbbing Python of Love Robin Williams or Sensitive Doctor Robin Williams?

What would the world be like if men were the ones who had to wear high heels and tight skirts?

Do you believe the expiration dates on food you buy? What sort of margin of error do you work within?

Do you think cows are mad that we take their milk? (Issue to consider: how you'd feel if a cow took your milk)

Describe the scene that led to someone eating the first oyster—do you think humans watched animals doing it first?

Do you think that the first time corn ever popped it scared the hell out of the Indians?

Would football be different if women were the referees? Boxing? Hockey?

? ¿ ?

"The very powerful and the very stupid have one thing in common. Instead of altering their views to fit the facts, they alter the facts to fit their views."

—*Doctor Who*

? ¿ ?

If you could play one professional sport, what would it be? What product would you receive an endorsement contract for?

Name five male figure skaters or gymnasts who you can say without a doubt are "straight."

Who's smarter, dogs—who chase their tails and drink out of toilet bowls—or cats—who lick themselves until they cough up furballs and chase shadows?

Is it really believable that the castaways on *Gilligan's Island* were lost for so many years on that "uncharted desert isle" after only "a three hour tour"?

Would the show have been as popular if it was called *Beverly Hills 90210-6227*?

If Ellen played a lesbian who was also a witch raising a wacky family of cute but loveable kids on her own, do you think her show would still be on the air?

More realistic: *Melrose Place* or *Three's Company*? Better written?

If Old Mr. Roarke (Ricardo Montalban) fought New Mr. Roarke (Malcolm McDowell) in a grudge match, who'd win? What about the Old Love Boat Captain (Gavin MacLeod) and the New Love Boat Captain (Robert Urich)? Captain Kirk (William Shatner) or Captain Picard (Patrick Stewart)?

Which of the seven dwarves do you most relate to? If you were the eighth dwarf, what would your name be?

Who's the best boss—Tony Danza (*Who's the Boss?*), Mr. Burns (*The Simpsons*), Mr. Spacely (*The Jetsons*), or Larry Tate (*Bewitched*)?

Didn't Samantha Stevens notice anything on *Bewitched* when Old Darrin (Dick York) was replaced by New Darrin (Dick Sargeant), or was the fact that both actors were named "Dick" confusing?

Who's the best mom—Carol Brady (*The Brady Bunch*), Roseanne (*Roseanne*), or Endora (*Bewitched*)?

Who's the best pet—Lassie (*Lassie, Come Home*), Dino (*The Flintstones*), or Astro (*The Jetsons*)?

Who was shackin' up with whom on *Gilligan's Island*? On *Star Trek*? On *The Love Boat*?

Were the *Dukes of Hazzard* kissing cousins?

? ¿ ?

"It takes a smart man to know when he's stupid."

—*Barney Rubble*

? ¿ ?

Was Mr. Roarke God?

Who would drive you crazy faster—Barney, Urkel, Mr. Rogers, or The Nanny?

Why don't men sit down when they urinate? Is it a "macho" thing to see how well they can aim? It would certainly make bathroom floors a lot cleaner (especially at night), and would give them time to think and relax. Would it make a difference if only men were allowed to clean bathrooms?

Why do women go to the bathroom in groups? Why don't men? Why don't women read in the bathroom?

If you started a band, what would you name it? If you were the lead singer and had only one name (i.e., Cher, Sting, Madonna), what would it be?

If hell was being locked in a waiting room with one person for eternity, who would be your hellmate? Whose hellmate would you be?

Whom do you know that is most likely to be or to have been possessed?

If you lived in a house that was haunted by a poltergeist or possessed in any manner, would you stay until the wall started bleeding or your daughter was sucked into a vortex, or would you get out while the getting was good?

If you fell in love with a person whose picture you saw in *National Geographic,* would you marry him or her, or do you think the ten-inch earlobes, full-body tatooing, and plates in their mouth would get in the way of your having a meaningful relationship?

? ¿ ?

"To succeed in the world it is not enough to be stupid, you must also be well-mannered."

—Voltaire

? ¿ ?

Do animals think we're magical gods, or just nuts?

√ If you could invent a holiday, what and when would it be? What special traditions/celebrations would take place on your day?

If you could live out a recent dream, which one would it be? Would it be a flying dream or a passionate dream?

If you could bring one character to life from your favorite book, who would it be?

If you and your dog could understand each other for just one minute, what would you say to it? What might it tell you?

If you were to be eaten by a giant insect, which one would you rather be eaten by?

If you had control of the *Starship Enterprise* for a week, what would you do with it? Where would you go?

Why don't the seats on the *Enterprise* have seatbelts, or airbags, or at least some automatic force field contraption?

Which of the Brady sisters would be most likely to have gotten pregnant as a teen?

If they were making an Afterschool Special about your life, what would it be called and who would you want to play you? (your friends, family?)

Who would you rather have for a judge, Judge Wapner, Judge Ito, or Judge Judy?

Who would you rather have as a lawyer, Johnny Cochran, Matlock, or Perry Mason?

Where do you think the "cool people" are—in heaven or in hell?

? ¿ ?

"So far as I can remember, there is not one word in the Gospels in praise of intelligence."

—*Bertrand Russell*

? ¿ ?

If you could be forgiven for one sin or really bad thing that you did, for which thing would you ask forgiveness?

If you could live one day over, which one would it be? Why? What about one year?

If you could eat only one food for the rest of your life, which food would it be? What about one restaurant?

Would you rather go sky diving, rock climbing, hang gliding, or bungee jumping?

If you only had six months to live, what would you do with your time? Would you do something outrageous and different, or keep living your life as it is?

If you were married and wanted to have children and there was a way to safely make men pregnant, who would carry the child to term? Who would complain more? (Issues to consider: primary breadwinner, ease of finding maternity clothes)

What would the world be like if we had to select our careers at age ten? Would the world be better or worse off? (Issues to consider: the prevalence of firefighters, ballerinas, cowboys, and astronauts; personal satisfaction and happiness)

If you could have one superpower, what would it be and how would you use it? (You don't only have to go with the usual powers—make up your own if you wish. Example: SuperSmell, SuperSarcasm, SuperStress, SuperHumor)

If you were psychic, do you think you'd join the Psychic Friends Network, or would you use your powers for something more meaningful that didn't involve Dionne Warwick?

If you could make either Barbie's clothes, Barbie's dream house, or Barbie's car into a life-size, usable version, which would you enlarge? What if you had to keep it that hot pink color?

If you could use a Barbie doll as a voodoo doll, who would you hurt and what would you do to them?

? ¿ ?

"It's better to keep your mouth shut and give the impression that you're stupid than to open it and remove all doubt."

—*Rami Belson*

? ¿ ?

If they made an action figure of you, what gimmick would you have? (i.e., kung fu grip, removable head, pull string)

If you could trade lives with anyone at all, would you do it and whom would you trade with?

If you could trade clothes with anyone at all, would you do it and whom would you trade with? What about trading bodies?

If a dead relative appeared to you and told you to give up all your earthly goods and go live on an island in the Caribbean to achieve eternal happiness, would you go? What if this dead relative was known for his/her practical jokes?

If you could take back something you said or did once, what would it be? Is there anything you'd like to say or do again?

If time is money, how much is a day worth? (Remember: The average human doesn't live for much longer than 26,280 days.) How much do you make every day?

What do you do with all those free labels non-profits and other charitable organizations send you in order to guilt you into making a donation? Is it wrong to use them without paying up, or are they just askin' for it?

In a bar fight, would you be more inclined to break a beer bottle to use it as a weapon, or to pick up a stool and crack it over your opponent's head?

If you had a theme song, what song would you pick? What if the song were played every time you entered a room or walked down the street? Would this change your choice?

At a urinal, is it wrong to look down? In a stall, is it wrong to talk to the person next to you?

When video phones become ubiquitous, do you think we should be able to blur our identities like they do on those cop video shows? Otherwise, how could we make crank calls?

If the one person you hate most in the world needs a kidney transplant, and you are the only person with a healthy kidney who is a perfect match for that person, would you give up your organ?

If you learned that you could save the life of one person in another country simply by agreeing to eat only calves' liver for a full year, would you do it?

Do you want your funeral to be a somber affair or a big party with lots of food and music? (Issues to consider: how much you want people to cry, how much you want them to enjoy it)

If you were at an early stage of your pregnancy and learned that your child was going to come out with the head of a dog, but was otherwise going to be normal, would you give it to the pound? (Issues to consider: What if the "dog child" someday becomes a bridge between the animal world and ours? Is dog food cheaper than baby food?)

Would you like to know the precise date and method of your death? What would you do to plan for it? What would you wear?

? ¿ ?

"It is only the wisest and the stupidest that cannot change."

—*Confucius*

? ¿ ?

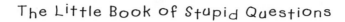

Which is worse: a paper cut or a skinned knee?

If you could be invisible for an hour every day, what would you do during that hour?

Is it more embarrassing to burp in public, to fart in public, or to walk around with your fly open?

Would you rather be David Copperfield (who is married to Claudia Schiffer) or John Stamos (who is married to Rebecca Romijn)?

Would you agree to be abducted by aliens and undergo experimentation if they promised you could "take the saucer for a spin" anywhere you wanted, and that you'd be home in time for dinner?

Who's scarier, Marilyn Manson or Charles Manson?

Would you rather be a butterfly or a cockroach? (Issues to consider: lifespan, aesthetics, durability, cuisine)

What would you say as your "last words" if you were about to be executed? Remember to keep it short and simple.

What would you order for your final meal? (Issues to consider: heartburn, allergies, preparation time)

Who would win a deathmatch between a nun and a Buddhist monk? (Issues to consider: use of rulers as weapons, martial arts expertise)

Who would be more likely to win a poetry slam—Shakespeare, Kerouac, or Milton?

If you were on *Star Search*, what category would you compete in—singer, comedian, actor, or TV spokesmodel?

? ¿ ?

"Nothing in the world is more dangerous than sincere ignorance and conscientious stupidity."

—Martin Luther King, Jr.

? ¿ ?

If you could perform a duet with any singer you wanted on national TV, whom would you pick and what would you sing?

If you were kidnapped, what would you consider to be a reasonable ransom? Do you think your loved ones would "pay up" or try to ambush the kidnapper, putting your life in danger?

Who would win a fight between Freddy and Jason? Would anyone? After all, they both keep coming back to life.

What color of shag carpet best describes your personality?

Would you rather be hunted by a pack of wild animals or by a group of men? (Issues to consider: militia groups, sharpness of teeth, food chain)

Would you rather be bled by leeches or burned with a hot poker in order to "get the evil out"?

If you were God and wanted to create a strange hybrid creature (like a platypus), what would you create? Why do you think God created the platypus—was he smoking something from the Garden of Eden?

When you close your eyes, are you seeing black, or are you not seeing at all?

Do you think there's a really poor country somewhere in which "toe cheese" is a delicacy?

? ¿ ?

"Bravery and stupidity go hand in hand."

—David Summers

? ¿ ?

If extraterrestrials visit our planet regularly, do you think they're offended that we never visit them?

What do you think is the correct way to fend off a shark attack?

If you had to defuse a bomb, how would you choose between the red wire, the blue wire, and the yellow wire? Would you try to make an educated choice, or simply do "eeney, meeney, miney, moe"?

If you were being tortured for information, do you think you'd talk, or would you be able to withstand the torture?

Is stealing office supplies from work any different from shoplifting?

If you were an evil mastermind trying to take over the world and you had just captured James Bond, would you place him in an unnecessarily complex deathtrap out of your line of vision (utilizing, say, a slow-moving laser or a slow-moving platform that lowered him into a pool of piranhas), or would you just shoot him yourself?

If you were in the process of escaping from a highly guarded prison with heavily armed guards, and you had just knocked one out, would you take his/her gun, or would you consider it a liability? (Issues to consider: while it might protect you, guards might be more inclined to shoot you if they see you're armed)

Is James Bond a sex addict, or just a slut?

How many times in life should you have to take your driver's test?

Given the choice between being a highly successful professional magician, a highly successful professional ice skater, a highly successful professional clown, or a highly successful professional exercise guru, which would you select, assuming they all received the same level of compensation?

Do you consider yourself to be more of a head-butter or a groin-kicker?

Do you ever find yourself avoiding lines or cracks in the sidewalk? What about avoiding ladders? Crossing against the light and looking both ways? Not eating food that has dropped on the ground? What other silly superstitions do you still believe in?

Do clowns ever have bad days at work? What do you think they do to cheer themselves up—or do they just go get drunk?

If you were in a horror movie, do you think you'd be one of the unwitting victims, or one of the people who survives?

In your circle of friends, who is most like Archie? Reggie? Jughead? Betty? Veronica? Chandler? Ross? Joey? Monica? Rachel? Phoebe? Jerry? Elaine? Kramer? George?

In a beehive, would you be the queen bee, a worker bee, or a drone?

? ¿ ?

"Some scientists claim that hydrogen, because it is so plentiful, is the basic building block of the universe. I dispute that. I say that there is more stupidity than hydrogen, and that is the basic building block of the universe."

—*Frank Zappa*

? ¿ ?

What is sexier—the *Victoria's Secret* catalog, the *Sports Illustrated* swimsuit edition, or a copy of *Playboy?*

If you could have safe sex by puffing out your cheeks during climax and then yelling "boogalaboogalaboogala-HA!", would you use this method, or would you be afraid your partner would find it too distracting and go with the more standard and commonly accepted methods of birth control?

If by simply downing a can of spinach you could temporarily bring superhuman strength to any part of your body, which part would you select?

Do you think the alphabet is in the right order, or should all the vowels be together? What about the letters "Q" and "U"? Are there other changes you'd make? Should punctuation marks be included? Sing your new alphabet song.

Why do you think the word "monosyllabic"
has five syllables, "abbreviation" is such a
relatively long word, and "onomatopoeia"
sounds nothing at all like what it is? Can you
think of better words for each?

"A word to the wise ain't necessary—it's the
stupid ones that need the advice."

—Bill Cosby

Would you rather have a life preserver under your seat on an airplane, or a parachute? After all, the seat cushions may be used as a flotation device.

Would you rather be sitting next to someone really obese on an airplane flight, or somebody really talkative? (Issues to consider: The talkative person might be annoying and the obese person might leak over into your personal space, but if the window next to you exploded then the obese person might plug it up)

Why do some people get to ride those carts in airports and others have to hoof it? Shouldn't you be able to rent one out, sort of like an airport taxi?

Which job is harder—flight attendant or waiter? Remember, flight attendants have to know what to do in case of an emergency, but waiters have to deal with a much larger menu selection.

Why do people who use "correct grammar" sound like such dorks?

How comfortable are you with the "auto pilot" that flies planes? Would you let your car be driven by "auto driver"? Remember, this isn't like cruise control where you still have to steer the car—the auto pilot's doing everything.

If they can make a "black box" that is so indestructible that it survives a plane crash, why don't they just make the airplane out of the same material?

Why do you think one of our most popular and sweet-sounding lullabies, "Rock-a-bye Baby," is actually about a serious case of parental neglect (a child who is living inappropriately atop a tree) and a life-threatening accident that ensues? What was Mother Goose thinking? Would you have let Mother Goose baby-sit your child?

What are curds and whey? What is a tuffet? Did Miss Muffet leave her curds and whey behind so the spider could eat them?

Would you rather have a peck of pickled peppers, a pie baked with four-and-twenty blackbirds, or a "Christmas Pie" with plums in it? Also, how was Peter Piper able to pick a peck of "pickled" peppers? Wouldn't you have to pick the peppers before you pickled them?

If you were Superman and someone threw a sixteen-ton weight at you, would you duck or just let it bounce off?

Do you think Wonder Woman ever gets cold in that outfit of hers? And isn't her invisible plane pretty dangerous to be flying around with all the air traffic these days?

Which superhero is most likely to be gay— Superman, Batman, Robin (The Boy Wonder— yeah, right), Captain America, or the Flash?

Does Ironman wear any undergarments beneath his suit? How does Superman shave? What does Batman do when he has to go to the Bat-room?

Do you think that superheroes could benefit from a little therapy? After all, most of them have some serious issues—abandonment, megalomania, suicidal tendencies, fear of intimacy, and burnout, to name a few.

Do you think that kids who are raised by two gay or lesbian parents have a difficult time "coming out" to them if they realize that they're heterosexual?

Should the "Department of the Interior" be called something more appropriate, since it deals with the outdoors and the environment?

Why do we have no problem believing
scientists when they tell us that there are
billions and billions of stars in the universe
(even though only a few thousand are visible
to us on any night), but when a waiter gives
us a plate of food and announces "careful—
it's hot" we always have to touch it to be sure?

Whom do you know that is most likely to
have been abducted by aliens? Most likely
to be an alien? (Issues to consider: spaced-
outness, frequent disappearances, desire
to travel)

What do you think it feels like just before you spontaneously combust? Is it more like heartburn or a really strong tickle?

Do cannibals prefer to eat different parts of people, or is a hand just as tasty as a foot?

Do foreigners understand English better if you speak to them using their accent?

What is your least favorite type of body hair?

Is it wrong to take a magazine from your doctor's or dentist's office? What about from an airplane? What if you leave a magazine behind in exchange?

Which is the better job: toll taker or garbageman?

Are there as many bad doctors as there are bad waiters?

"Don't call me stupid!"

—Otto (Kevin Kline,
A Fish Called Wanda)

Where do forest rangers go to "get away from it all"?

After they eat, do amphibians have to wait
one hour before getting out of the water?

Which muppet are you most like: Ernie, Bert,
Cookie Monster, Grover, Kermit, or Big Bird?

About the Author

David Borgenicht is a writer, editor, and part-time stupid philosopher who lives in Philadelphia with his wife, who is not at all stupid. He is the co-author of *Mom Always Said, "Don't Play Ball in the House" and Other Stuff We Learned from TV* (Krause), and the author of *Sesame Street: Unpaved* (Hyperion), as well as the forthcoming book, *The Jewish Mother Goose* (Running Press). When he's not thinking up stupid questions, he's usually doing something inane anyway.

- What do your friends say about you when you're not around?

- If you could create a new animal by combining already existing one, ~~who that~~ which ones would you combine & what would you call it.

10/23 — 5:00

$9.95 paper
ISBN 1-887166-28-9
160 pages • 5¾ x 10
Humor/New Age

Enlightening strikes again.

Doing away with all earnestness and doctrine of whatever stripe, Swami Beyondananda, author of *Driving Your Own Karma*, has never metaphysical question he doesn't like. Here, he elaborates on his theory that life is actually easy, in fact, it's Duck Soup (an expression that even pre-dates the Marx Brothers and means "fun, easy, a piece of cake").

Hysteria books are available at book and gift stores everywhere, or by calling 630-961-3900.

A new cartoon collection from nationally syndicated "Sylvia" cartoonist Nicole Hollander, featuring inscrutable felines of impeccable taste. Cats who think too much, cats who plot dastardly deeds but get distracted, cats who hypnotize their owners, cats obsessed with food, food, food. A veritable kitty feast!

$9.95 paper • 1-887166-43-2
112 pages • 6 x 6 • Humor

Hysteria books are available at book and gift stores everywhere, or by calling 630-961-3900.

Comediennes, humorists, film stars and other famous women provide quips for all occasions.

On Ego: "Listen, everyone is entitled to my opinion."
—Madonna

On Exercise: "My grandmother started walking five miles a day when she was sixty. She's ninety-three today, and we don't know where the hell she is."
—Ellen Degeneres

$7.95 paper • 1-887166-38-6
144 pages • 5½ x 7 • Humor/Quotations

Hysteria books are available at book and gift stores everywhere, or by calling 630-961-3900.

"I don't think so!"

The Inner Bitch calls it as she sees it. Author Elizabeth Hilts heralds an end to Toxic Niceness and arms women with the highly effective phrase, "I don't think so," which she applies with grace, wit and humor to myriad situations.

$8.95 paper • ISBN 1-887166-44-0
112 pages • 5½ x 8½ • Humor/Self-Help

Hysteria books are available at book and gift stores everywhere, or by calling 630-961-3900.